Synapse Symphony

N. Bonfanti

ISBN: 978-1-927914-25-0

Published by Flower Press
Montreal, Canada

I dedicate this collection to my most honest critic
and devoted supporter, my mother, Patricia

Running Current
If the current carries you to hungry-bellied pythons
hiding
beneath the lily pads, awaiting rocks to trip you
then
let God guide your feet
If you find yourself reaching us in darkness, then
light for us a candle,
so that we all may see

In Hew of This
You know your world's in trouble when your
politicians cry
fighting civil war although it causes them to die
now our pride is overcome with hate so viral
infecting the old, as young, taught to lead this
upheaval
of the life we knew; of the life that we knew
worked
of the hope to prosper, hope our freedom is
preserved
hypocritical their words, attacking the only honest
"We only want to help"; only for power are they
earnest

The State or Our Disunity
Am I such an anomaly?
A solo in the band?
Christian in astronomy?
The only question, lone raised hand?
There must be another who knows, another who
cares
There must be lovers
Of humanity and justice and political affairs
Wickedness preys on ignorance, because the art
Of ignoring comprises our whole world
Trust in place of knowing; knowledge here
Would ring absurd
Let us stumble, let us fall, so we can see how the
ground looks
It is ever rising and our skies,
Laid out to crooks
If dust – dead cells from the living, decay of what's
been built –
Is the first symptom of death for all
All/each disjointed as a quilt
Then where is your warmth?
Tell me where's your stronghold?
Invested in a mortal whose destruction lives forever
Let us shiver in this cold
Encourage vigilante by condemning those not tried
Who will protect? Who will lead?
When bills are used for greed and our own power
takes a side
Ok, ok, ok, now progressive groups hate me
I'm k, and k, and k if I dare disagree
Do you know? Your new-found fortune has a price
Lice are those who eat at others – illness is
vulture's vice

I hope my job will be there when I wake up here
tomorrow
I hope what I've invested is not repaying what
they've borrowed
I hope the price of needs has not tripled as
previously
I hope my grandbabies do not grow up in poverty

Less Miserable
If the water doesn't take me, I'll drown within the
air
So thick and stank and angry
Takes the perm right out of your hair
A picture on the wall- no – a mural of tragedy
Some stop and stare – none have care. We all think
we don't see
My check last week was fit for food
Today: a digit's gone
"mistake" I told payroll, and then she said: "there's
nothing's wrong"
My daughter caught me crying; "an onion" I said
I'd cut
To bed she fled; to keep her warm, her door I
quickly shut
The pan – I used to catch the rain – I needed not for
meals
The cupboard empty, the fridge turned off – my
daughter's dad now steals

Unwell Affair

If you want to sit, sit; not just the weary need the
rest
Those who work so hard, feeling that building in
their chests
From the running that they do and the paper that
they chase
The pasts that they run from, that they wish they
could erase
So sit on the bottom God has given you for free
If you find food for your mouth, I commend you for
the skill
To beg and cry until your pity's spread; those
passing give bread
everyday for you the same
every night I love the rain, for I know what I plant
will grow
as you search for shelter and you pray that it won't
snow

Evolution of Knowing
Somewhere between birth and death, we must learn
Otherwise there is no point
Anoint those equal us as gods – simply because
we're told
Much of the world is mad, because they haven't
learned
Have you yearned to know the truth of your roots?
Uncouth to teach what is not proven: "the world has
made itself"
Now, look at your health
By chance there's ways to heal
Never let me feel a doubt of this – it's real
Can real be touched? Can touch be kneeling?
To what? Rise if you're the highest "being"
I'll never see you move
Somewhere in the desert – far – you'll find the
lesser fools
If no books - no tools - exist, then look upon the
moon
Look upon the child who has grown inside a womb
Look to the dirt, look to the sea; reflections you'll
behold
Look upon what's perfectly made by earth's most
complex mold
Never let us look upon the lie that's ever told

If we have been so blind with vision
2020, let us now humble our mind,
knowing our knowledge is of
Nothing

Perspective
Perfume masks the stench of your rotten teeth
From the vile
You spit up
Maybe the lies feel better in your stomach
Until you've had enough
Should a taste be acquired for the sour in what's
real?
Or should the truth be sugared
Since we can't palate what's congealed?
Is it sin if it's for good?
Was it sin with Robin Hood?
Depends on if you ask the rich or poor
Interchange the two, for what one has, the other
lacks
What shines more?
The mist reflecting in your eye, or
Gold when sun seeps through the cracks?

Is he too old or she too young?
Depends who benefits more
Once each cup's too full to pour
And in each heart is space for pain
To reach each wall, echoing the
Irrevocable "cure"

Branches
None as misunderstood as he: the tree
He needs to breathe, but how ashamed are we
To stifle it. We cannot see – beyond – to its roots
Put simply: it's the proof
That connects it to the heavens, as created as us all
The tree of life
On it, living were sacrificed
To bring wisdom with its fruit – knowledge
Let us show how
Little we know
End the life of a perfect Lord
Upon His masterpiece:
The tree
Let the branches choke the life
Of those lesser than "ourselves"
None is lesser than a man who steals
Breath
Because the complexion of
The flesh on the bones – Is not fair
– we think we're fair?
Fair is not what life is – but is Fair death?
Death finds us all – even the tree
Fair or not? Never fair – it never will be

Ode to Those Who are Not Well
Time: Chases me
and I don't notice, until it's swallowed all my
movement
Never will I prove it
Because no one else can SEE!
It's a whole conspiracy
So unworthy of the air we breathe - we
inhale and leave as though we owe nothing
when skills fade, crave better pleasure
while all other ventures
now just feather at the ends
as they, too, fade to memories of "then"
Defy rules if we can't follow - claim failure's our
choice!
Voice says "I'm in control" but the power
In the hands is hollow
The walls encase our house - now crumble
"I wanted more sunshine" Heat-stroke now
dazes all that was steady
I just needed to be humble
TIME: chases me
and I don't notice, until it's swallowed all my
movement
Never will I prove it
Because no one else can SEE!
It's a whole conspiracy

When the air moves, I panic
Is it just me?
I shake when I'm angry
And I think my fist is Iron
I yell upon the wall for causing my hand to bleed
As I lose my Iron
noises hurt - people sting
But rationale won't touch me

Cough into the wind - we all inhale another dust
And at the hush of the world, one's own heartbeats
drive him MAD
"You never understand me. Understand me!
Understand me!"
I feel this way. Can't you see? When I feel this way,
I cannot see.
TIME: chases me
and I don't notice, until it's swallowed all my
movement
Never will I prove it
Because no one else can SEE!
It's a whole conspiracy

The poison runs through us - It is poison because it
burns
In the urns - the bodies can be lost in a breeze -
where I wish to be!
To no longer be alive, but still be here able to see
The ailments of the flesh are so accustom now -
being ill is being well
White-clothed clerks give medicine - they only
wish
to sell - to be rich
To be rich: I don't know what this means
Put us in a bottle - document responses
To the hell you put upon us
Just to pay back your deposits
On a government-funded study
"Crazy People" is the synopsis
TIME: chases me
and I don't notice, until it's swallowed all my
movement
Never will I prove it
Because no one else can SEE!

It's a whole conspiracy

My mother says I'm crazy - but I'm the only one
who's sane
I'm not crooked, can't you see?! I'm just in a
crooked frame

Pretend
It's a trunk, and it's sealed and its purpose is to hide
a character so ugly; act a part, tricking your mind
If it's you your soul lies to, your own heart being
mismanaged,
Can another save you, or must you be labeled
"damaged?"

Kite
Let it fall, if your kite won't fly
It must need to touch the ground, No shame
In seeing what no longer is, hearing where there is
no sound
And no one sings
Only shame is if you're still holding to the strings

Gravity
Blowing on a feather, expecting it should fall
Like the bricks holding my foe
As though fire should not glow
And my blindness is my own
Further, yet, I wander, fathoming its weight
Pressing my own against this gate

The Ever-known Feeling of Failure
How it feels to be sick within one's self
of one's self, towards one's self
To be tearing one's own self out from behind his
skin
to be released from the captivity of his
transgressions.
How it must feel if one could be free from
his thoughts, his memories, his shame
To be banished from this world and delivered into
nothing
Nothing wrong, nothing ugly, nothing persisting in
its illness
Nothing meaningful, nothing beautiful, nothing
learned.

Aspiration
A symptom of a cancer of the mind
succeeds to make you spiritually blind
Cuts your motor lines -
Now, all you can move is your hope –
from existent, to impossible to find
Blood washes the sky just before the night
commandeers the atmosphere
Into the sheer cloud your eyes journey to the end of
the knowledge
that can be sought from earth
At the hearth of the fire is the image you aspire
To emit; burn bright, as you hope your legacy will
glow, as the sky before the night
How it is washed with blood – burning but never
lost - as a stone

Quite Simply
I have no children, have no lover
Have little in ways of another
Have no pictures on the wall
Almost have nothing at all
I have a tongue; it knows its place
If not, pencils, so words erase
I have a ladder, to appear tall
and grass beneath in case I fall
I have a sun; it watches me
I have a God to see
what His son can't see
I have dirt, I know by heart
It tires me, how it smiles at me, as if it's smart
I have a yearning, but to flee
and finally, a bus ticket, adios
my simile; adios
my metaphor; adios
my apostrophe; adios
allusions and illusions interfering with me

Iterate
Don't warn me the water is deep
I can swim
Not like a fish, like a shark; those in my path lose
limbs
My hands apart from pens, are still
I'll speak your heart to death, dizzy you from
listening, make your mind ill
So, don't warn me of the steepness of this hill, or
The expenses of this bill; nothing bought or sold
exceeds
Things built and told
These words will reach the level of attack,
reverberate distances
And back
Turning those hills to dust, and parting waters as
With Moses, Jesus was
My hands need no labor; the message is the product
Laborious for some to hear; always
To rest near
Never
To run nor disappear

Rhetorically Seeking
Did I cause your loss of sight or did you never see
at all?
Are you shrill, or nil of words
like when I hear birds call?
your thoughts hush; your bones rust
your flesh to dust, and its needs turn lust
can you write something, truly, that the ink has
never seen?
Or, is your pen leaking;
is your paper lit, or is it burning?
Rhymes are not in need
though, your prose must bleed
of metered timing
absent of rhyming
otherwise it is just writing - just to read
Let the true poet speak; let her words dance
Through her mouth, she breathes, in a rhyme trance
You're in a mind trance
If you let her words halt your chatter,
Hitting your conscious like a batter,
metaphors fall mute
then never will you prosper
even if your foe's a brute -
a beast without a language
I sympathize your anguish
for the talent that you lack

After Inspiration
After inspiration's spent, morning feels like night
The darkness is depressing, otherwise it is too
bright
It hurts your eyes to see, and your lungs tire from
air
Tight is your chest in water; thinning is your hair
You've spent the money that you made
Accomplished what is expected
And cannot what you hoped
At some point, all connected
Is your world, and boring and slow
Gone are all your friends, unreachable and mute
Weary is your body, hobbies
Intangible for you

It is now when there is nothing
But to rest beyond the grave
When your spirit is relieved
And your soul, finally is saved

Witchcraft
As a cheetah to a zebra:
So does earth devour

Here, Satan rules – the prince
Of darkness – we must overcome
Night vision
Strength from the heavens – when his claws
Around us, grasp
The power of "no"
I will pay no mind to lying tongues

Never will I fall and never
Can I run
Do not change where you reside; alter your
residence
By casting out the devil
Diligently ignite your candles – do not
Let them go out unwatched
Nor let angels of fire creep through open windows

An excuse for all your failings: "the devil can't be
won by mortals"
How wrong are you
When the Word of God lies at your bedside?
Dust-covered crisp, whole pages

Ice in a pot stirred by a mere witch
Scratch at the itch
As your veins resist
The burn of the cold creeping inside you
Is it harmless if I watch?
Is it harmless if I chant?
Is it harmless if a man places his hands inside my
pants?
Is it harmless if I drive, when I can barely see?

Let the tree dodge me
For, life is just a harmless trance

Depend
Mine, all mine, and I'll never let you go
From this prison cell
In which you dwell
alone
Back-peddle – plea freedom from the life you alone
chose
I am fading, I am weak
Feeling I may leave
"Please go, give me reprieve"
But you'll miss me so
As you scratch, as you tear, even your flesh you'll
sacrifice
Your family - you don't know, and it doesn't bother
me
They just make the time go slow, waiting 'til you I
get to see
Let the steel doors shut, your body is all I need
In my greed, I hold
onto the one
silently praying to be freed

Singeing Sanctity
Evening skin with evening sin, ready to burn up the
day
The way one would if tomorrow were wood
Soaked in gin
Rotting in to decay
Let it simmer this summer – which will start with a
blaze
A brush fire
The "brush" is the good
Hummer the bird won't sing once it's heard
Nor the chime of the chirp from the chip of his beak
will join
In the ruin of the work of his God

Seeking Smoldering Sin above Spiritual Salvation
Surrounded by the flames approaching – tortured
By the screaming of the smoke alarm
In my ear
I see my flesh fall from my bones
Dissolving in a heat I cannot
Feel – I must
Be cooled by the touch of my tear
Surrounded by decay my eyes can't meet
The smoke stings them closed, as it
Finds my nostrils – I hold
My breath to shut it out
'til finally I gasp! Again and again
My throat: it chokes
The thunder is so looming in chaos
That called it here
The building falls and disappears as soon
As it hits the ground without a wince
Of fear, without a sound
Without a shriek; without a care
As if it wants to leave its life on earth
My life is here
On earth
But it's pushing me away – asking me to leave
I'll stay, I'll stay, until you drag me from this pit
Of hell, I'll stay
You take my challenge, I realize as you tug my
molten arm
Grab around my waist and lift me
From the flame I'm sitting on
My clothes are gone
My hair is dust, my breath is long
To the afterlife, I come?
You place me on the earth, that's calm
"Daddy?"

"Shh, my dear, it's done"

Service
Locks – brown and thick - join the dusty tiles
The mechanical bee around my ears exposes my
scalp
High and tight – a chill tonight while I sleep almost
bald
The morning seems to be racing toward me – let its
engine stall
Let my dreams linger; let the darkness call
The vibration on my head so soothing
I nod, and then I wake
"Stay with me" he says as he wields the tool
"I would hate to slip"
The strands stick to my fingers as they fall away
A couple strays reach my toes, perspiration drips
I don't recognize myself – I know the change won't
be reversed
I will never be the man I was, if I survive a man at
all
My identity has fallen and is swept into the trash
"Fifteen"
I drop a twenty. Money won't serve me well
At home, the quickest night begins – I dream of hell
My pillow's firm without my hair
I feel breezes through the open door
Onto a trip of thousands of miles
Onto – into – war

Nativity and Pains
Tidy tinsel trolling through the tree
Love and lace is lighting up
My home on Christmas Eve
Presents packaged, pretty and pale
Pastels and whites against a deepest green
The deepest green is he who loves a gift that can be
held

Cookies, cakes, and cranberries
Collard greens and pie
Dancing down my gullet 'til I think I'll explode and
die
Sifting, sorting, season's settings
Nativity and canes
Warmth and winter – opposites
As happiness and pain

Ever erasing early embers
Of a Christmas cheer
Is looking across the table's dressing
At my father's empty chair

Loneliness
It's so heavy, so thick. My strength is vanishing
cold as brick; lies on my skin atop my body
Suffering and there's no stopping.
It's crushing me; it's all I hear
Like the roaring of a bear, the humming of an
engine
the melody unclear.
The silence of a home - empty
In my twenties, and I've aged so quickly
I feel caged; sickly
And I know there is no cure.

Transparency
Cut through each vein of this composition, 'til my passion's bled
If you still don't see my truth, then color my hands red
But when the rain falls, and it snows
I'll glisten and I'll glow
As white as words Christ himself said
With a heart as soft as clouds, heavy as lead
Heavy for the children with no water and no bread
Their bellies may be full, but their minds within are hollow
Burning brimstone and coal, is their desire to see and follow

Soul's Mate
I'm in the un-holiest matrimony with the music of
my mind
In love with writings I create and a clock that tells
no time
Is this what it means to have your mind sound?
Mine drowned
in daydreams
the shore was ugly and the surface thick with hate
though the earth is muddy,
the heavens above rain as majestic
as the melody held captive in my soul

Orectic

In the morning, my eyes find empty sheets
and a lack of heat
I'll go back to dreaming, so I'll never lose you

I have my eyes closed, and I feel you
Your skin is soft, but you're firm
I can hear you
Your breathing is deep, as an engine humming
enabling the movement of the machine you are
running
You're stunning
I open my eyes to see yours
Skin darker than mine, eyes lighter
I can hear the lighter click on within you
Igniting the look you shine on me
You move within and out of me
With my legs tight around you, I beg you be still
Stay deep, stay close, stay here, don't leave
Then you breathe
Into me; my mouth swallows the chill
You never look at me outside of this room
Yet now, locked on me, stare at me,
"Get on me"
"I will"
For you, my body always complies
I hear you purr, no, a growl
"Come'er"
Your voice deeply, almost strained
I can hear your pleasure
In the few words you're saying
"You feel good; you're so sexy"
You're flattered and smile
I haven't been kind in a while
Because I've felt you won't let me
This is truly the only moment my heart yearns

To be close, to be noticed, to be still in the night
To lie naked, your skin, sweating into mine

Honey Suckle
Crystal blue water running violently over smooth,
grey rocks,
as if racing to be free from the dirt walls that hold it
Crashing and thrusting with captive cries
efforts proven vain
A small figure looked upon the pitiful waves
sympathetically, for her situation paralleled theirs
Her restless loins yearned for the comfort of the
outside world,
for experiences beyond the metal wall that held her
Iron-framed eyes caught hers through the chain-
links,
teasing her to taste the fruit blossoming beyond its
bounds
Thunder groaned disapprovingly at her sorrow.
"I'm sorry," she cried, "don't be so upset."
Genuine pleads to an unyielding jury
In her heart, she knew the consequences
But she ignored the warnings of her father
selfishly feigning a deaf ear.
Bare feet trampled through the healthy grass
ripe honeysuckle temptingly leaned toward her side
of the fence.
It's okay if I take it;
it's natural for it to be picked.
"It's not my fence; it's my father's,"
Her hands so soft, like the silk worms nestling
beneath her toes
Hands not tainted with the blood of men,
Hands ready to pluck the innocence from the
pasture
Her lips closed tightly around the flower
so tightly that no breath could penetrate through
The sweet dew dripped slowly over the cravats of
her white dress

and seeped through the fabric until saturated
The girl's once faithful covering was now thrown
though the
dirt until resembling coal
Branches of the plant gripped her and delivered her
to the earth
Vines wound themselves through her legs
and released the refreshing rain across her body
Skin, gently kissed by the sun, roughly tossed by
the earth
For hours she stayed, as weeds found their way to
her

Demise of The Fly
So patiently, she waits
Her beauty – unmatched
So elegant, she looks; so poised
Her colors: vibrant; her lips make no noise
She draws him with her scent; she's warm deep
inside
Just moistened enough for drowning small minds
Not thinking, he enters. Oh, what a death
To be buried in flowers – Venus' nest.

Settled
Cursed to be beautiful
Cursed to be a wed
To a man who will never satisfy her bed

Cursed to be chosen
Cursed to be him
With few dollars, much lust, and
Impotent limbs

Grown
I was sitting on the bus; there were, maybe, a few of
us: women
I on one side, she across, others stood
Should
I desire to be noticed by a boy, it wouldn't take
much
Effort to draw him. With his baggy jeans and chain
causing a slouch
I can picture what he'll look like at forty with that
posture –
Mixed with substance overuse, perhaps?
Not full-out abuse; I'm not saying he has a
problem, of that sort
At least
It's amazing to me how it won't take much to get
this boy
He'll stop for anything easy
Believe me
And she'd be – you know
The girl sitting across from me
But he likes a challenge when he walks, holding up
his jeans
Shoes untied, dodging laces
Paces slowly
Mouth shiny with metal and cut glass, looks like
braces
And when he talks? As if he's never been taught
English
He speaks louder when he's near her, so she'll look
Women aren't worth approaching; just let her
notice you
Earrings are big and gold and costume
Cheap is as cheap looks
A bustier complete with hooks
But it's called a shirt; who wears that?

More skin revealed than covered, nails acrylic, hair
is colored
I sit across and watch
He turns toward her like he knows her – he knows
her type:
Misguided, taste-and-tried, and
used
Is never hit never abused?
Never loved is what she'll choose, when she
doesn't give much
To get a boy
Recognize a man; be a woman

Sideways on The Straight and Narrow
A magnetic field of trouble, and you're stuck in
the middle
of a dust cloud forming that will blind you
discontentment is your weakness, and it holds your
life
as a beam of sand,
crumbling beside you
goal on a golden scroll that is soldered shut
Intentions burnt; hope is prodded and bled out
The aroma of a goddess and it passes through the
dirt
Stunning in a fragrance, catching fragments of the
earth
From birth to heaven, I see a path that's straight;
yet, you stray - apart
From the direction of its gate
A clock you beg to run, while it makes you wait
Impatience is your downfall, dominating in this
stage
Frustrating read - so many pages- in this life so long
Can't stand still - please stay strong
Strengthen your will - heaven's so far, you kneel
Your legs tire from their stance - now the dirt you
feel
Infected by the soil, only rising, now, will heal

Journey
Here: in between somewhere
Is it better to be knowing all that is near
or to be knowing that far, there is more than what is
here?
De-fragmenting is the bridge behind - beyond is
where I bear
To take a step
Toward something greater
maybe worse - never to reverse
the path yonder; yonder is where I steer
It is not by knowing that we guide to a higher chair
To sit and rest
in a glorified lair, but
knowing is by seeing, and all
I've ever seen does not compare to
what rests in the somewhere surrounding
here

The Cleanse
The child with a challenge - the devil sought him
out
Helpless with an illness and a mother not devout
God can heal this child, but faith
like age
comes only when you're ready
His body is bloody; she's told he'll stain her hands
"His pain won't end; he won't live"
Who are we to say?
"His illness to you, he'll give"
Just take him away
Remove those who are sick
They'll all want it this way
Those who don't pray; who from us stray
End their pain; save our own
"Clean" tomorrow here today

It's Called: Death
He's soliciting attention in the subtlest of ways
Hidden by haze
in a night covered by dust
This gentle soul's in lust
Yearning to touch, or be touched; love, or be loved
Not knowing above
His head is rising a halo that
Will crush him – a fog to drown him
Below grounded
I wish I could reach out – I can but he's too far
To reach him
It's growing dim
As the moon begins to flee – can no one bear
To witness this but me?
Feel it; you won't admit he's touching you
We don't want to be called wrong – this time
I'm running from,
not toward others
It bothers us, doesn't it? When someone turns
Away from what we socially accept
I'll stay with him; this boy who's
Called a speck
Before he's learned to speak, his mouth open
In a shriek
In the night, hidden in sight, his light
Shines so brightly that we're blinded
By and from what we chose never to seek

Angel
I saw an angel yesterday; this morning, it was gone
I saw an angel, and I didn't understand
I asked to be let be
T'was mere epiphany, imaginary, not real,
not to me
I feared the being's intent
Majestic - heaven-sent was he.
I couldn't understand I asked to be let be.
Once vision returned to me, my angel whence had
fled
Never to be seen again. I saw an angel yesterday.
This morning it was gone.

www.ingramcontent.com/pod-product-compliance
Lightning Source LLC
Chambersburg PA
CBHW021118020426
42331CB00004B/536